365 Ways
to Love
your Cat

Also by D. H. Love from Random House Value Publishing:

365 WAYS TO LOVE YOUR LOVER

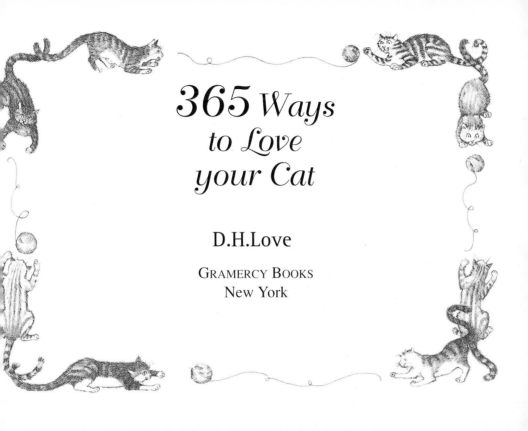

365 Ways to Love your Cat

D.H. Love

GRAMERCY BOOKS
New York

This 2000 edition is published by Gramercy Books™, an imprint of Random House Value Publishing, Inc., 201 East 50th Street, New York, NY 10022, by arrangement with the author. The Copyright of the Book shall remain the exclusive property of the copyright owner.

Gramercy Books™ and design are trademarks of Random House Value Publishing, Inc.

It is not the intention of the author or publisher that you should follow any instructions concerning the care of your cat other than those of your vet.

Printed in Malaysia

Random House
New York • Toronto • London • Sydney • Auckland
http://www.randomhouse.com/

A CIP catalog record for this title is available from the Library of Congress

ISBN: 0-517-18275-0

8 7 6 5 4 3 2 1

Introduction

Some cats are long-haired and some are short-haired, but all seem to share certain immewtable characteristics. If you are a cat lover or a cat owner (the two usually go together) here is a handy little guide filled with helpful tips and advice on how to love, cherish and respect (and sometimes spoil) your feline friend 365 days of the year.

If you have a cat already, sit back and enjoy. If you don't have one yet, you may be in for something quite delightful soon.

1  When you wake give your cat a morning cuddle.

2 Make sure you give your cat caresses throughout the day.

3 And spend some extra time tickling around the ears and under the chin.

4 Let your cat rub up against you – even if you are wearing black.

5   When your cat winds her way through your legs, she is saying you are part of her territory, so be calm and collected and let her do her thing.

6   *Don't forget to buy your cat a special toy of his own.*

7   A ball of yarn or a toy scented with catnip will give your cat hours of frolicking fun.

8   *Spend quality time playing with your pussycat – at least twice a day.*

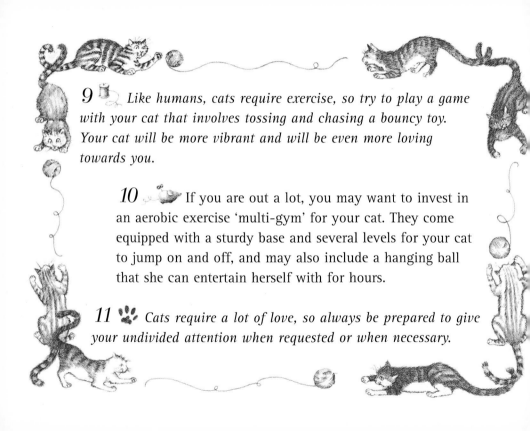

9 *Like humans, cats require exercise, so try to play a game with your cat that involves tossing and chasing a bouncy toy. Your cat will be more vibrant and will be even more loving towards you.*

10 If you are out a lot, you may want to invest in an aerobic exercise 'multi-gym' for your cat. They come equipped with a sturdy base and several levels for your cat to jump on and off, and may also include a hanging ball that she can entertain herself with for hours.

11 *Cats require a lot of love, so always be prepared to give your undivided attention when requested or when necessary.*

12 Be generous at 'cat-time' and rub her tummy often.

13 *Don't forget to make your lap available on a regular basis.*

14 Be your cat's biggest fan.

15 *Always remember the essence of Cat-tesian philosophy: 'I am, therefore you must love me!'*

16 On the practical side, always keep your cat's food bowl clean.

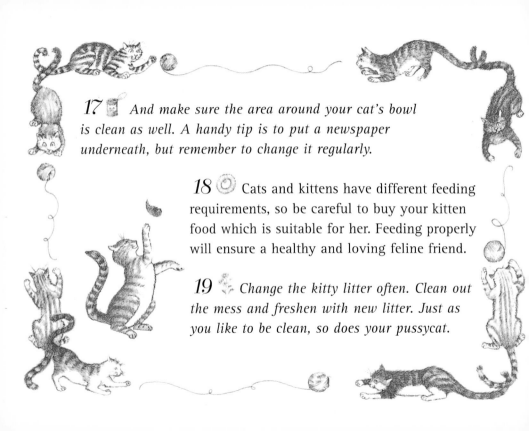

17 And make sure the area around your cat's bowl is clean as well. A handy tip is to put a newspaper underneath, but remember to change it regularly.

18 Cats and kittens have different feeding requirements, so be careful to buy your kitten food which is suitable for her. Feeding properly will ensure a healthy and loving feline friend.

19 Change the kitty litter often. Clean out the mess and freshen with new litter. Just as you like to be clean, so does your pussycat.

20 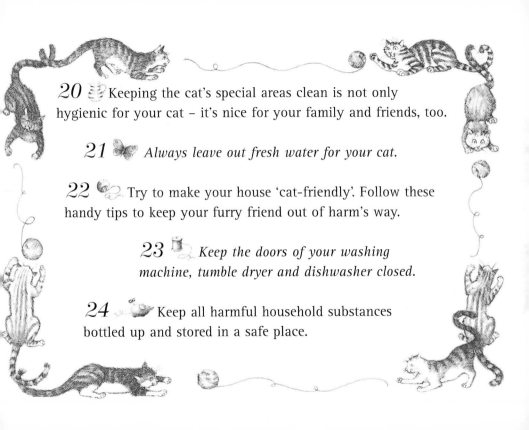 Keeping the cat's special areas clean is not only hygienic for your cat – it's nice for your family and friends, too.

21 *Always leave out fresh water for your cat.*

22 Try to make your house 'cat-friendly'. Follow these handy tips to keep your furry friend out of harm's way.

23 *Keep the doors of your washing machine, tumble dryer and dishwasher closed.*

24 Keep all harmful household substances bottled up and stored in a safe place.

25 *Don't leave poisons such as slug pellets where your cat might find them.*

26 And keep poisonous plants out of nibbling range.

27 *Don't ignore your cat's persistent cries. It could be something serious that requires the vet.*

28 If your cat exhibits unusual behaviour or anything out of the ordinary, bring it to the vet's attention.

29 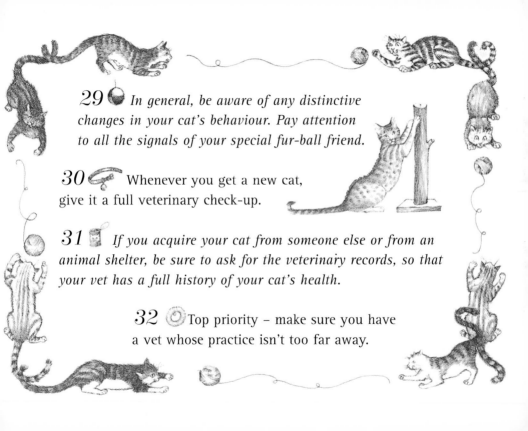 *In general, be aware of any distinctive changes in your cat's behaviour. Pay attention to all the signals of your special fur-ball friend.*

30 Whenever you get a new cat, give it a full veterinary check-up.

31 *If you acquire your cat from someone else or from an animal shelter, be sure to ask for the veterinary records, so that your vet has a full history of your cat's health.*

32 Top priority – make sure you have a vet whose practice isn't too far away.

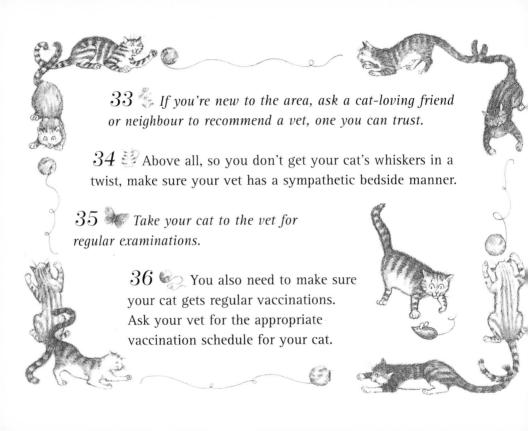

33 *If you're new to the area, ask a cat-loving friend or neighbour to recommend a vet, one you can trust.*

34 Above all, so you don't get your cat's whiskers in a twist, make sure your vet has a sympathetic bedside manner.

35 *Take your cat to the vet for regular examinations.*

36 You also need to make sure your cat gets regular vaccinations. Ask your vet for the appropriate vaccination schedule for your cat.

37 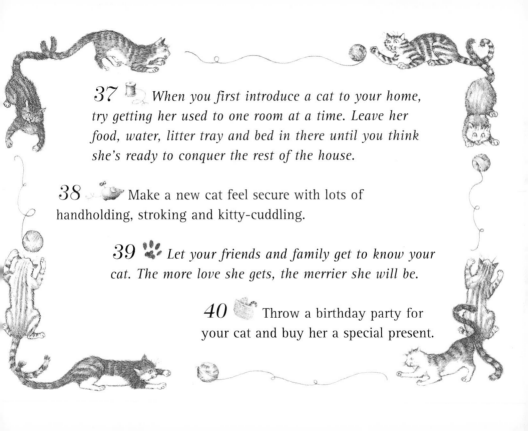 *When you first introduce a cat to your home, try getting her used to one room at a time. Leave her food, water, litter tray and bed in there until you think she's ready to conquer the rest of the house.*

38 Make a new cat feel secure with lots of handholding, stroking and kitty-cuddling.

39 *Let your friends and family get to know your cat. The more love she gets, the merrier she will be.*

40 Throw a birthday party for your cat and buy her a special present.

41   *Why not decorate the house with party balloons and streamers for the occasion?*

42   And when it's your birthday, don't forget to include your cat in the festivities.

43   *Loving your cat means never having to worry about a cat-astrophe.*

44   Never raise your voice to your cat.

45 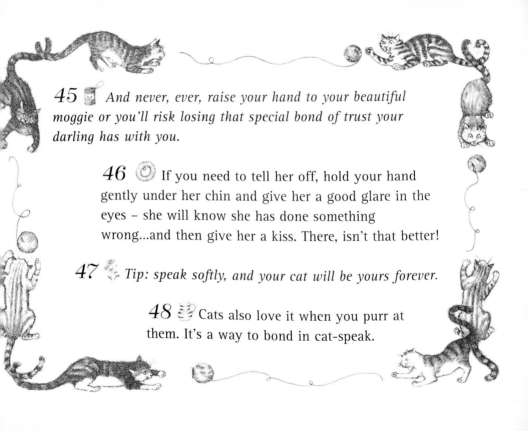 *And never, ever, raise your hand to your beautiful moggie or you'll risk losing that special bond of trust your darling has with you.*

46 If you need to tell her off, hold your hand gently under her chin and give her a good glare in the eyes – she will know she has done something wrong...and then give her a kiss. There, isn't that better!

47 *Tip: speak softly, and your cat will be yours forever.*

48 Cats also love it when you purr at them. It's a way to bond in cat-speak.

49 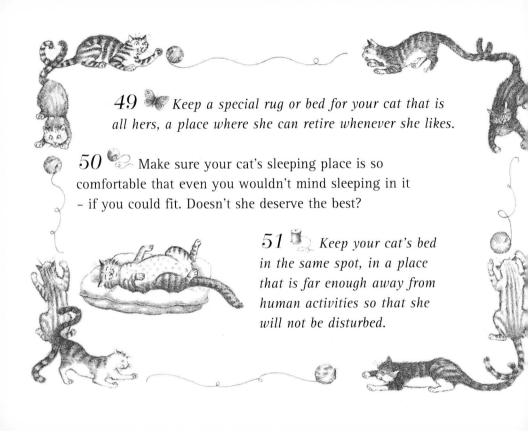 Keep a special rug or bed for your cat that is all hers, a place where she can retire whenever she likes.

50 Make sure your cat's sleeping place is so comfortable that even you wouldn't mind sleeping in it – if you could fit. Doesn't she deserve the best?

51 Keep your cat's bed in the same spot, in a place that is far enough away from human activities so that she will not be disturbed.

52 If you have a cat that loves the outdoor life, it's a good idea to have a cat-flap so that your cat can come and go as she pleases.

53 *If you have a cat who is new to cat-flaps, you may need to train him how to use it. Try to entice him with some fresh fish on the other side of the door.*

54 If your cat has been outside, make sure she's clean when she comes in and has no leaves or thorns stuck to her coat or paws.

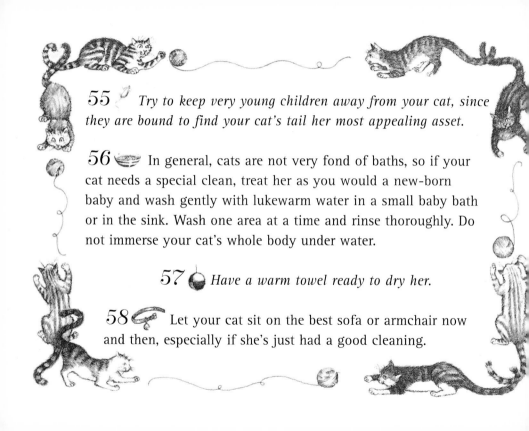

55 *Try to keep very young children away from your cat, since they are bound to find your cat's tail her most appealing asset.*

56 In general, cats are not very fond of baths, so if your cat needs a special clean, treat her as you would a new-born baby and wash gently with lukewarm water in a small baby bath or in the sink. Wash one area at a time and rinse thoroughly. Do not immerse your cat's whole body under water.

57 *Have a warm towel ready to dry her.*

58 Let your cat sit on the best sofa or armchair now and then, especially if she's just had a good cleaning.

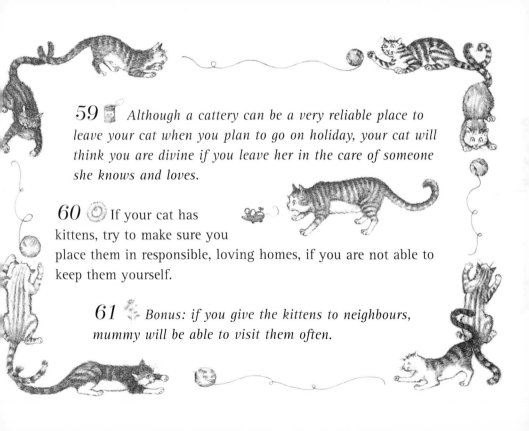

59 *Although a cattery can be a very reliable place to leave your cat when you plan to go on holiday, your cat will think you are divine if you leave her in the care of someone she knows and loves.*

60 If your cat has kittens, try to make sure you place them in responsible, loving homes, if you are not able to keep them yourself.

61 *Bonus: if you give the kittens to neighbours, mummy will be able to visit them often.*

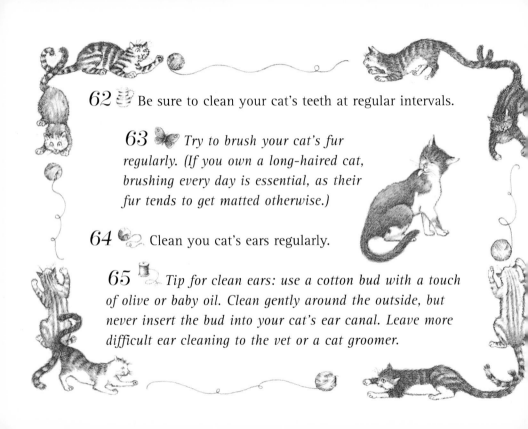

62 Be sure to clean your cat's teeth at regular intervals.

63 *Try to brush your cat's fur regularly. (If you own a long-haired cat, brushing every day is essential, as their fur tends to get matted otherwise.)*

64 Clean you cat's ears regularly.

65 *Tip for clean ears: use a cotton bud with a touch of olive or baby oil. Clean gently around the outside, but never insert the bud into your cat's ear canal. Leave more difficult ear cleaning to the vet or a cat groomer.*

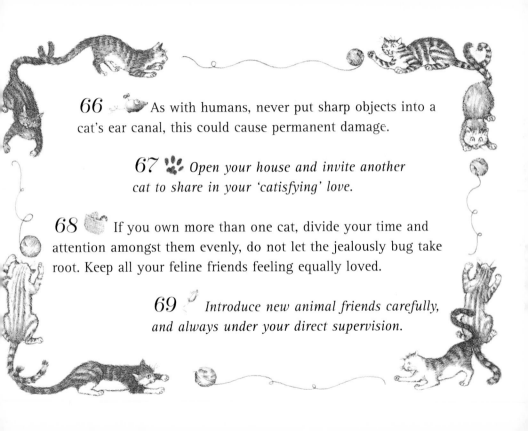

66 As with humans, never put sharp objects into a cat's ear canal, this could cause permanent damage.

67 Open your house and invite another cat to share in your 'catisfying' love.

68 If you own more than one cat, divide your time and attention amongst them evenly, do not let the jealously bug take root. Keep all your feline friends feeling equally loved.

69 Introduce new animal friends carefully, and always under your direct supervision.

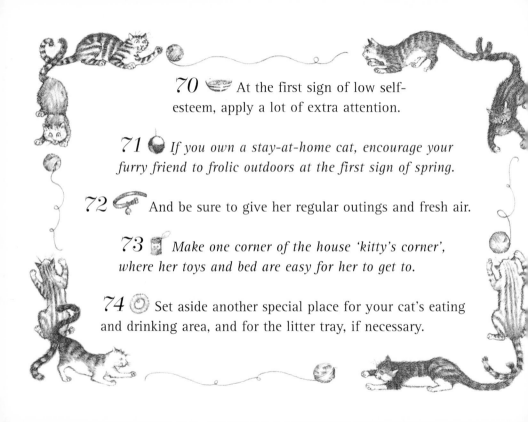

70 At the first sign of low self-esteem, apply a lot of extra attention.

71 *If you own a stay-at-home cat, encourage your furry friend to frolic outdoors at the first sign of spring.*

72 And be sure to give her regular outings and fresh air.

73 *Make one corner of the house 'kitty's corner', where her toys and bed are easy for her to get to.*

74 Set aside another special place for your cat's eating and drinking area, and for the litter tray, if necessary.

75 *Buy a cushion or flat pillow for your cat to lay on when she's not frequenting her bed or yours.*

76 Create a safe area where your cat can lie in the sun all day if she wants to, far away from any open windows or balcony ledges.

77 *If you take your cat on holiday with you, make sure she is as comfortable as she is at home.*

78 Never show your neighbour's cat more attention whilst in the presence of your own.

79 🧵 *In general, don't flirt with other people's cats.*

80 🐁 Do take your cat with you to visit the neighbours, if she is welcome.

81 🐾 *Buy or make a soft toy that your sweetie can play with – then she'll always have a ready-made playmate when you're not around.*

82 🧺 If your cat enjoys being cuddled, rock her to sleep on your lap.

83 🐟 *Stroke her as she's falling asleep.*

84 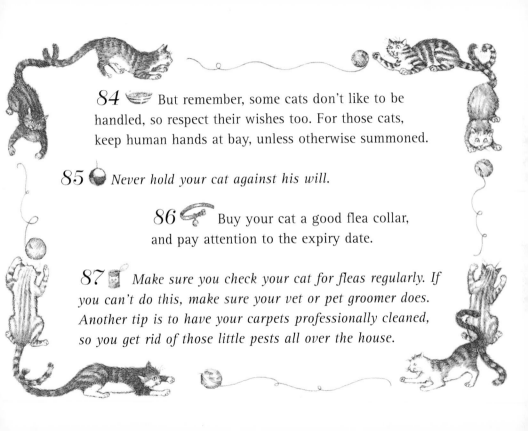 But remember, some cats don't like to be handled, so respect their wishes too. For those cats, keep human hands at bay, unless otherwise summoned.

85 *Never hold your cat against his will.*

86 Buy your cat a good flea collar, and pay attention to the expiry date.

87 *Make sure you check your cat for fleas regularly. If you can't do this, make sure your vet or pet groomer does. Another tip is to have your carpets professionally cleaned, so you get rid of those little pests all over the house.*

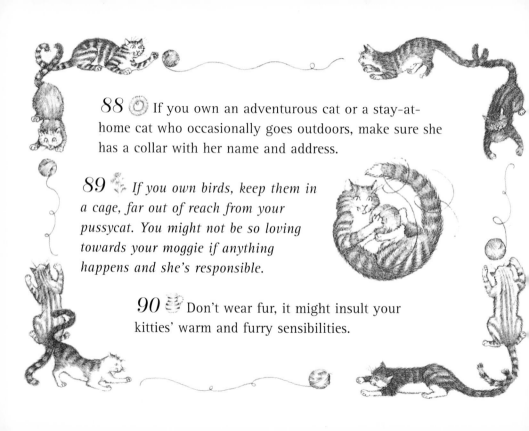

88 ◎ If you own an adventurous cat or a stay-at-home cat who occasionally goes outdoors, make sure she has a collar with her name and address.

89 🌿 *If you own birds, keep them in a cage, far out of reach from your pussycat. You might not be so loving towards your moggie if anything happens and she's responsible.*

90 🐚 Don't wear fur, it might insult your kitties' warm and furry sensibilities.

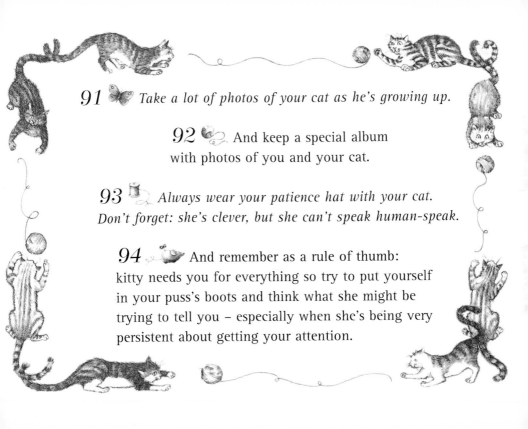

91 *Take a lot of photos of your cat as he's growing up.*

92 And keep a special album with photos of you and your cat.

93 *Always wear your patience hat with your cat. Don't forget: she's clever, but she can't speak human-speak.*

94 And remember as a rule of thumb: kitty needs you for everything so try to put yourself in your puss's boots and think what she might be trying to tell you – especially when she's being very persistent about getting your attention.

95 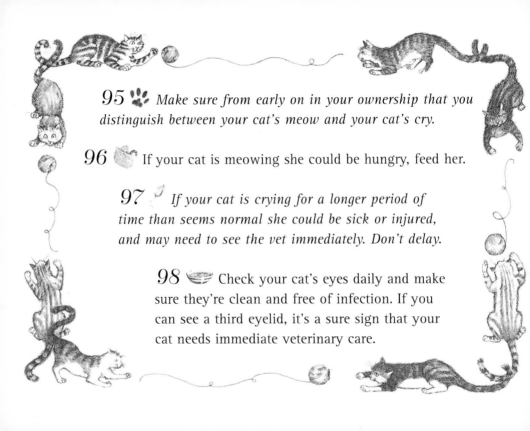 *Make sure from early on in your ownership that you distinguish between your cat's meow and your cat's cry.*

96 If your cat is meowing she could be hungry, feed her.

97 *If your cat is crying for a longer period of time than seems normal she could be sick or injured, and may need to see the vet immediately. Don't delay.*

98 Check your cat's eyes daily and make sure they're clean and free of infection. If you can see a third eyelid, it's a sure sign that your cat needs immediate veterinary care.

99 *Wash your cat's eyes with clean, warm water every day.*

100 If your neighbours own a dog, don't let your cat roam unattended, and make sure she has a tall tree nearby for a quick escape.

101 *Leave a night-light on when you go to bed, so that you don't make the mistake of stepping on her if you get up in the dark.*

102 Keep an eye on young children when your cat is within their reach.

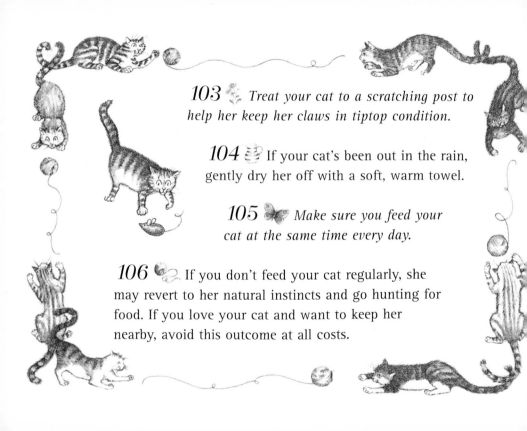

103 *Treat your cat to a scratching post to help her keep her claws in tiptop condition.*

104 If your cat's been out in the rain, gently dry her off with a soft, warm towel.

105 *Make sure you feed your cat at the same time every day.*

106 If you don't feed your cat regularly, she may revert to her natural instincts and go hunting for food. If you love your cat and want to keep her nearby, avoid this outcome at all costs.

107 *You don't like to eat the same thing day in, day out, so give your pussycat a choice selection of foods throughout the week. Don't be afraid to spoil her every now and again.*

108 Don't be annoyed when your cat sheds her hair all over your clothes. Think of it as a physical manifestation of her love!

109 *Cats have a natural grooming instinct. Let them groom in peace.*

110 Let your cat bask in the sun.

111 However, although it may sound funny, if your cat is fair-haired you may have to apply sun block cream. Ask your vet for advice. If you do apply any lotions, clean them off properly when the sun goes down.

112 If your cat is relaxing, don't disturb her quiet time.

113 If you are feeling fidgety, don't inflict your restless state onto your cat. In other words, don't nudge the cat.

114 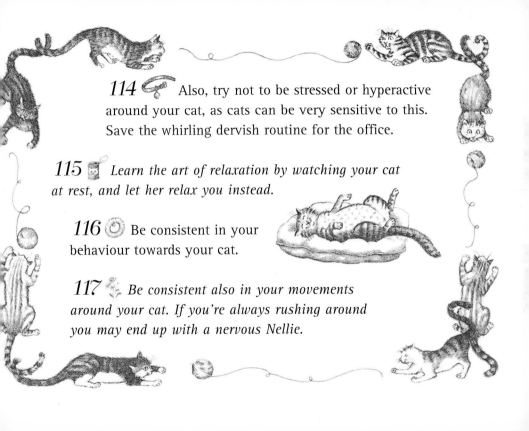 Also, try not to be stressed or hyperactive around your cat, as cats can be very sensitive to this. Save the whirling dervish routine for the office.

115 *Learn the art of relaxation by watching your cat at rest, and let her relax you instead.*

116 Be consistent in your behaviour towards your cat.

117 *Be consistent also in your movements around your cat. If you're always rushing around you may end up with a nervous Nellie.*

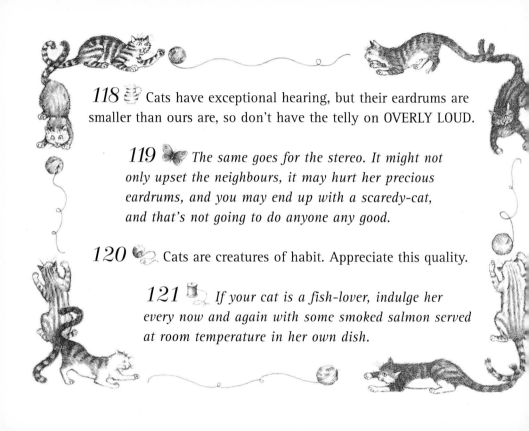

118 Cats have exceptional hearing, but their eardrums are smaller than ours are, so don't have the telly on OVERLY LOUD.

119 *The same goes for the stereo. It might not only upset the neighbours, it may hurt her precious eardrums, and you may end up with a scaredy-cat, and that's not going to do anyone any good.*

120 Cats are creatures of habit. Appreciate this quality.

121 *If your cat is a fish-lover, indulge her every now and again with some smoked salmon served at room temperature in her own dish.*

122 However, don't make it a habit of feeding your cat your food, or you'll truly spoil him. You want a loved cat, not a spoiled cat.

123 *Even though it may be tempting, because we equate food with love, do not overfeed your cat, or you'll have an overweight and possibly unhealthy feline on your hands.*

124 Don't expect your cat to help you with the housework, but do let her keep you company; she's very good at that.

125 *Don't buy leather furniture if you want to stay in an adoring, loving mood with your cat.*

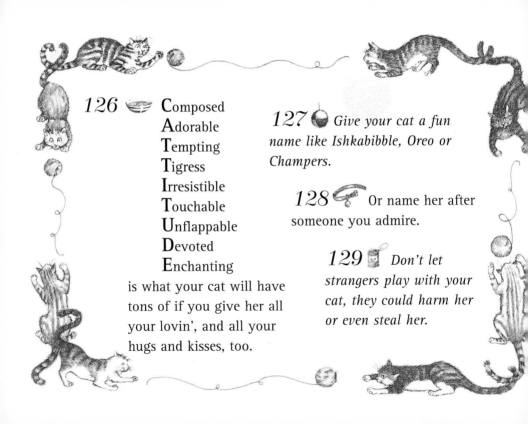

126 **C**omposed
Adorable
Tempting
Tigress
Irresistible
Touchable
Unflappable
Devoted
Enchanting
is what your cat will have
tons of if you give her all
your lovin', and all your
hugs and kisses, too.

127 *Give your cat a fun name like Ishkabibble, Oreo or Champers.*

128 Or name her after someone you admire.

129 *Don't let strangers play with your cat, they could harm her or even steal her.*

130 It's nice if your cat can have her own safe window sill to watch you from as you come and go.

131 *If your cat suffers from hair-balls, give her some fresh grass to eat; it will help her 'get' or cough them off her chest.*

132 Keep a diary of your cat's cutest antics. You needn't make an entry every day, but a chronicle of these life events will be a wonderful keepsake.

133 *Read your sweetie-cat bits of T.S. Eliot's* Old Possum's Book of Practical Cats *during tea-time and rediscover the magic.*

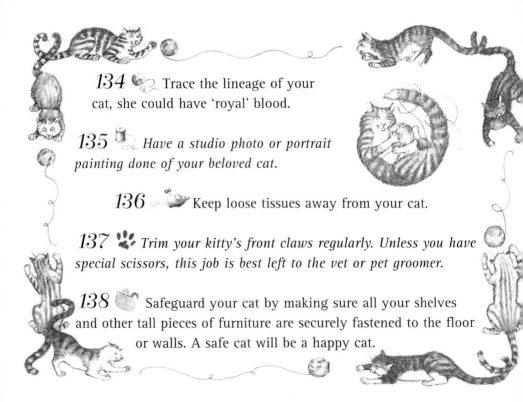

134 Trace the lineage of your cat, she could have 'royal' blood.

135 *Have a studio photo or portrait painting done of your beloved cat.*

136 Keep loose tissues away from your cat.

137 *Trim your kitty's front claws regularly. Unless you have special scissors, this job is best left to the vet or pet groomer.*

138 Safeguard your cat by making sure all your shelves and other tall pieces of furniture are securely fastened to the floor or walls. A safe cat will be a happy cat.

139 *And make sure your curtains are also secure on their rails. The same goes for blinds, since anything movable and heavy could hurt your cat if it was to fall on her.*

140 Always put kitchen waste in a bin with a secure lid, and if possible keep your bin in a cupboard. You don't want your cat to get sick from eating your rubbish.

141 *Most cats have a 'sweet-tooth' for fish, so keep your pet goldfish out of harm's way.*

142 Do not name your cat Fido, he might suffer an identity crisis.

143 *A visit to a pet psychologist may be worthwhile if your cat has a 'trying' pet problem that you and your vet just can't seem to solve.*

144 You have a hell-raiser for a pet? Cuddle, cuddle, cuddle, love, love, love helps soothe away the savage beast.

145 *Make your home their home.*

146 Treat your cats as if they were your children – with love, respect and affection.

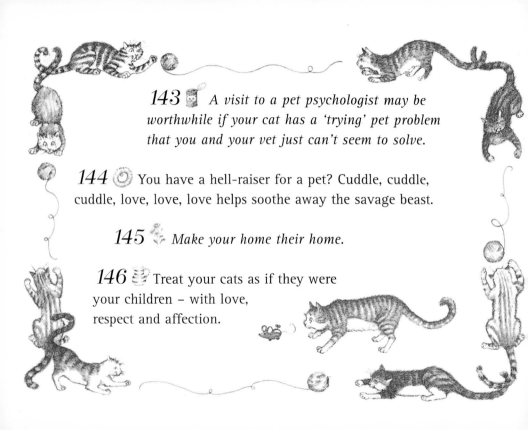

147 🦋 *Let your cats think they rule the house, they will be less spiteful when you're away.*

148 🧶 If your cat has had an 'accident' and left some mess, wash that area clean with warm water and soap.

149 🧵 *If you don't want your cat to do something he's already in the process of doing, try saying 'NO' in a very firm, but loving voice.*

150 🐭 Try not to pussyfoot around your cat; she'll know you're being indecisive.

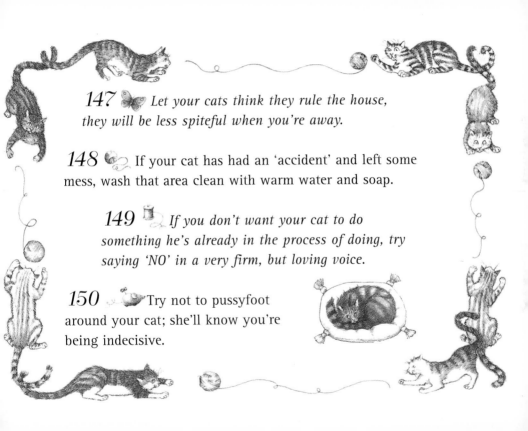

151 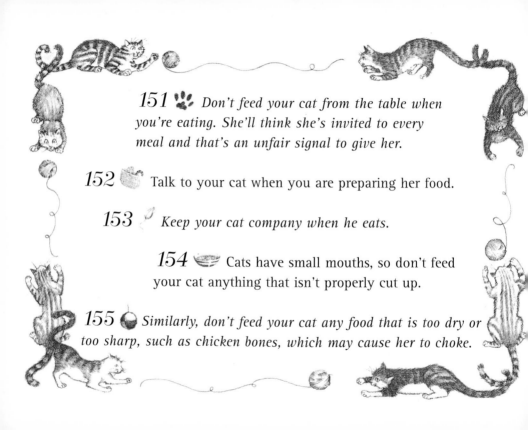 *Don't feed your cat from the table when you're eating. She'll think she's invited to every meal and that's an unfair signal to give her.*

152 Talk to your cat when you are preparing her food.

153 *Keep your cat company when he eats.*

154 Cats have small mouths, so don't feed your cat anything that isn't properly cut up.

155 *Similarly, don't feed your cat any food that is too dry or too sharp, such as chicken bones, which may cause her to choke.*

156 Don't treat your cat as an object; cats are individual, independent creatures who will choose to spend time with you if they feel like it. Respect their decisions.

157 *Cats are elegant creatures, therefore treat them with grace and dignity.*

158 Don't expect the mountain to come to Mohammed. A cat's affection will need to be won.

159 *If you are loyal, loving and respectful your kitty will reward you in kind.*

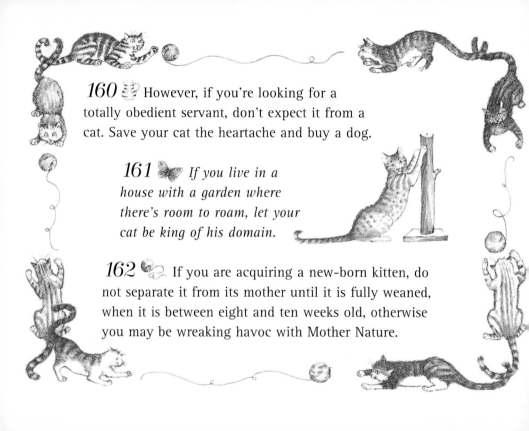

160 However, if you're looking for a totally obedient servant, don't expect it from a cat. Save your cat the heartache and buy a dog.

161 *If you live in a house with a garden where there's room to roam, let your cat be king of his domain.*

162 If you are acquiring a new-born kitten, do not separate it from its mother until it is fully weaned, when it is between eight and ten weeks old, otherwise you may be wreaking havoc with Mother Nature.

163 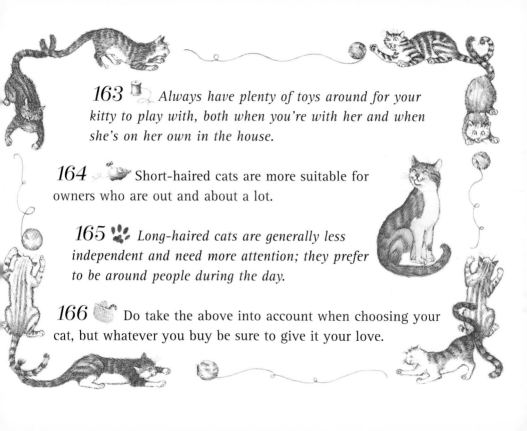 *Always have plenty of toys around for your kitty to play with, both when you're with her and when she's on her own in the house.*

164 Short-haired cats are more suitable for owners who are out and about a lot.

165 *Long-haired cats are generally less independent and need more attention; they prefer to be around people during the day.*

166 Do take the above into account when choosing your cat, but whatever you buy be sure to give it your love.

167 *Remember to always pamper, pamper, pamper, love, love, love.*

168 Don't try to compete with your cat's adventure outside the house – just make sure your cat feels nurtured and well taken care of inside.

169 *Because a pet is an investment, you may want to consider getting insurance, which can help reduce the costs of vet's bills over the long-term.*

170 If you are not prepared for frequent cat pregnancies and having to deal with kitten adoptions, it may be wise to get your cat neutered. Ask your vet about this.

171 When you're cleaning your cat's food bowl and any toy or object he puts in or near his mouth, don't use household disinfectants. These can be very strong and make your cat sick, just wash with unscented soap and water.

172 Keep small objects such as children's toys that a cat might eat or swallow, and possibly choke on, out of harm's way.

173 Remember a gentle hug a day keeps the nasties away.

174 Don't let your cat out to play if the weather is bad or if a storm is expected.

175 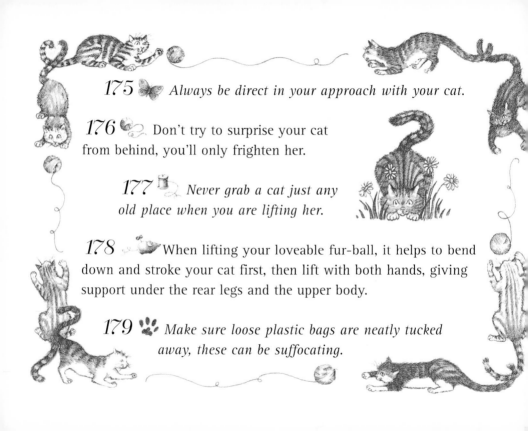 *Always be direct in your approach with your cat.*

176 Don't try to surprise your cat from behind, you'll only frighten her.

177 *Never grab a cat just any old place when you are lifting her.*

178 When lifting your loveable fur-ball, it helps to bend down and stroke your cat first, then lift with both hands, giving support under the rear legs and the upper body.

179 *Make sure loose plastic bags are neatly tucked away, these can be suffocating.*

180 Before your cat goes outside make sure all sharp objects, such as gardening shears, secateurs and scythes, are not left lying around in the garden.

181 Never leave your cat alone in the car on a hot day.

182 Never leave your cat alone in the car on a cold day.

183 Don't embarrass your cat by calling the fire brigade out to rescue her if she is stuck up a tree. Try to get her down yourself first – without risking life and limb.

184 With love and attention, your cat will be just...

Pretty
Unwavering
Robust
Rollicking
Famous (to you, of course)
Energetic
Co-ordinated
Terrific

185 *If you're having a loud party with lots of guests, keep your feline friends in a separate room away from clumsy feet and uneducated hands.*

186 Ask your vet which sorts of food are best for your cat at each stage of his life.

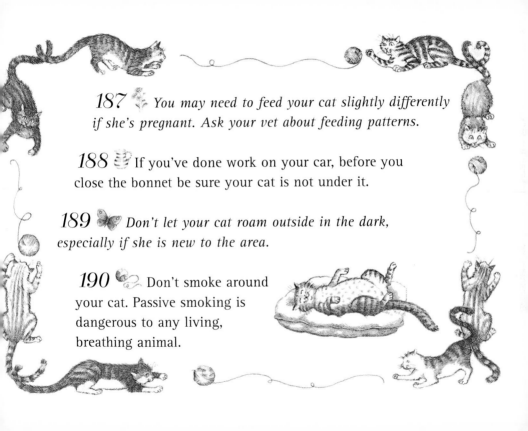

187 You may need to feed your cat slightly differently if she's pregnant. Ask your vet about feeding patterns.

188 If you've done work on your car, before you close the bonnet be sure your cat is not under it.

189 Don't let your cat roam outside in the dark, especially if she is new to the area.

190 Don't smoke around your cat. Passive smoking is dangerous to any living, breathing animal.

191 *Become an expert in reading your cat's signals from meows to hisses, and even spitting, and become even closer to your furry feline friend.*

192 Like a child, love and nurturing at an early age will help your cat develop with confidence into a confident animal.

193 *Stroking is vital to development.*

194 If you travel with your cat or take her to the vet, make sure you use a good quality pet carrier or a secure box with proper ventilation holes.

195 Never let your cat roam loose in a moving car as he could get hurt if you have to brake suddenly. When travelling by car, use a pet carrier secured by a seatbelt or placed firmly on the floor.

196 There's FUSSING and there's fussing. Don't over- FUSS over your cat.

197 Keep loose power cables in and around the house safely tucked away from your cat.

198 If you have an open fireplace, make sure the area is properly screened from little trespassers.

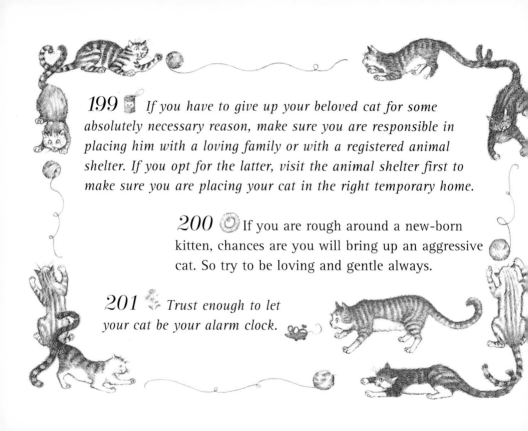

199 If you have to give up your beloved cat for some absolutely necessary reason, make sure you are responsible in placing him with a loving family or with a registered animal shelter. If you opt for the latter, visit the animal shelter first to make sure you are placing your cat in the right temporary home.

200 If you are rough around a new-born kitten, chances are you will bring up an aggressive cat. So try to be loving and gentle always.

201 Trust enough to let your cat be your alarm clock.

202 And while she may not be able to read, your cat will make the most wonderful bookend. Books are oh so comfortable to lay on, so give your cat the key to the library!

203 *Let your cat roll all over you; it's like having a masseuse in the house. Don'tcha just love your cat!*

204 Smile at your cat every day.

205 *The cat got your tongue? Loving your cat may make you speechless at times.*

206 Don't leave a new-born kitten alone in the house in the early stages of its life.

207 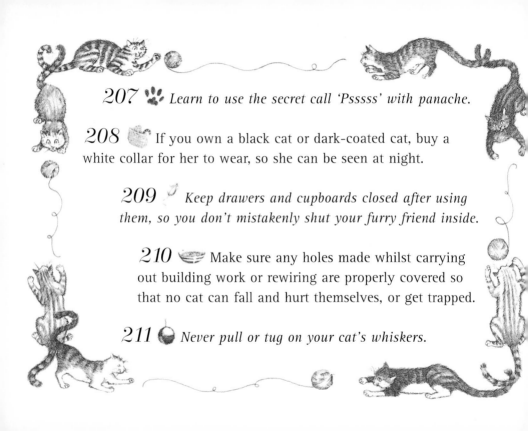 *Learn to use the secret call 'Psssss' with panache.*

208 If you own a black cat or dark-coated cat, buy a white collar for her to wear, so she can be seen at night.

209 *Keep drawers and cupboards closed after using them, so you don't mistakenly shut your furry friend inside.*

210 Make sure any holes made whilst carrying out building work or rewiring are properly covered so that no cat can fall and hurt themselves, or get trapped.

211 *Never pull or tug on your cat's whiskers.*

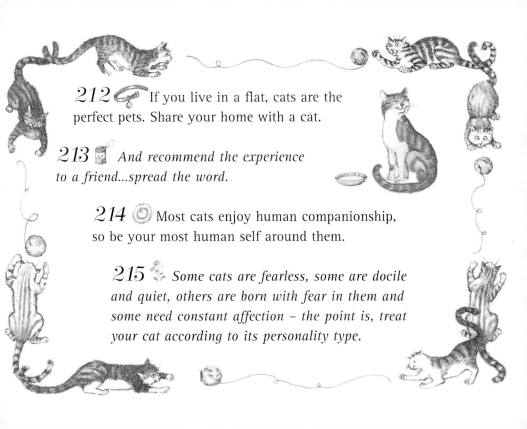

212 If you live in a flat, cats are the perfect pets. Share your home with a cat.

213 *And recommend the experience to a friend...spread the word.*

214 Most cats enjoy human companionship, so be your most human self around them.

215 *Some cats are fearless, some are docile and quiet, others are born with fear in them and some need constant affection – the point is, treat your cat according to its personality type.*

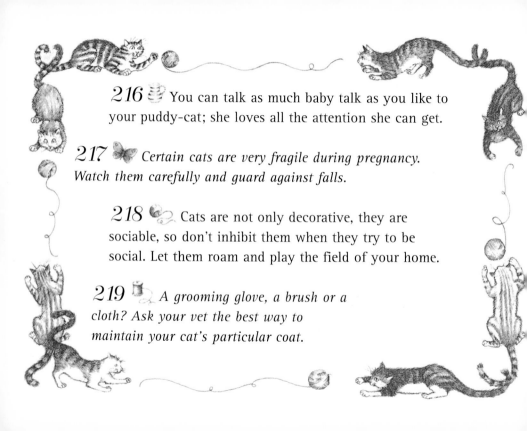

216 You can talk as much baby talk as you like to your puddy-cat; she loves all the attention she can get.

217 *Certain cats are very fragile during pregnancy. Watch them carefully and guard against falls.*

218 Cats are not only decorative, they are sociable, so don't inhibit them when they try to be social. Let them roam and play the field of your home.

219 *A grooming glove, a brush or a cloth? Ask your vet the best way to maintain your cat's particular coat.*

220 🐾 *Always show the proper*

*C*uddles
*A*doration
*T*reasure
*T*houghtfulness
*I*ndividuality
*Q*uietude
*U*nderstanding
*E*asygoing
*T*act
*T*astefulness
*E*xaltation

(that's cat etiquette to you)
when dealing with your cat.

221 🐦 Cats are very like humans and can suffer from arthritis too, so ask your vet about possible remedies for their pain.

222 🧺 If you are alone, instead of speaking to yourself, speak to your cat. She's a very good listener.

223 *Just as children, and some adults, become irritable if unwell, consult with the vet if your kitty shows increasing signs of irritability.*

224 If your cat's tail is drooping, make sure you bring this to your vet's attention.

225 *Be sure to keep your cat well groomed, since dandruff may give your friends and family an allergic reaction. If she's not clean, that might deprive your pussycat of a lot of extra love.*

226 Keep your house as clean from dust and dust mites as you can, as they may give your cat an allergy.

227 *Keep an eye on your cat's 'bathroom' habits, as this is often one of the first ways you can detect if something is wrong.*

228 Likewise, keep a watch on food and water intake, and if either is out of the ordinary, make sure you consult your vet.

229 *Check your cat's skin for any lumps, bumps or skin conditions that feel abnormal.*

230 The same goes for checking for nasty pests like fleas. Not every flea collar does its job properly.

231 *If mummy cat is pregnant, again don't fuss too much, as she instinctively knows what she needs and what she needs to do.*

232 Mummy cat needs peace and quiet to nurture her new kittens, make sure she gets this as a top priority.

233 *Keep a watchful eye out, but do let your cat play with the neighbourhood cats.*

234 You may want to consider getting another kitten or cat for your first one as a companion.

235 When introducing another cat into the house be sure the breeds go well together.

236 Cats are said to have nine lives, so make every one of them count to the maximum with pussy love galore.

237 Spend a rainy day at home with your furry friend.

238 And snuggle up together in front of the telly.

239 Do let your cat sleep with you every now and again, if this isn't already a part of your daily routine.

240 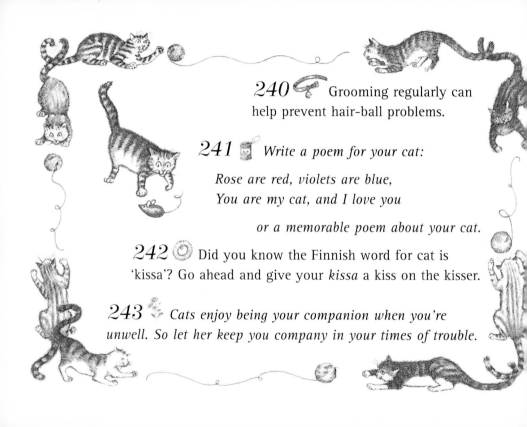 Grooming regularly can help prevent hair-ball problems.

241 Write a poem for your cat:

Rose are red, violets are blue,
You are my cat, and I love you

or a memorable poem about your cat.

242 Did you know the Finnish word for cat is 'kissa'? Go ahead and give your *kissa* a kiss on the kisser.

243 *Cats enjoy being your companion when you're unwell. So let her keep you company in your times of trouble.*

244 It may be safest to wait until your kitten is fully grown before you put a collar on her, for if the collar is not loosened as she grows bigger, she could risk choking as a result.

245 *Not every cat is confident. Spend your time coaxing a cat that needs security, and your time will be well spent.*

246 Treat your cat like a member of the family. I'm sure this goes without saying.

247 In an argument, always take your cat's side.

248 Only breed kittens if you know you can give them a proper home.

249 Make sure you follow precautions for de-worming your cat from an early age onward. Check with your vet when you need to do this.

250 It's not an old yarn, cats do like balls of old yarn.

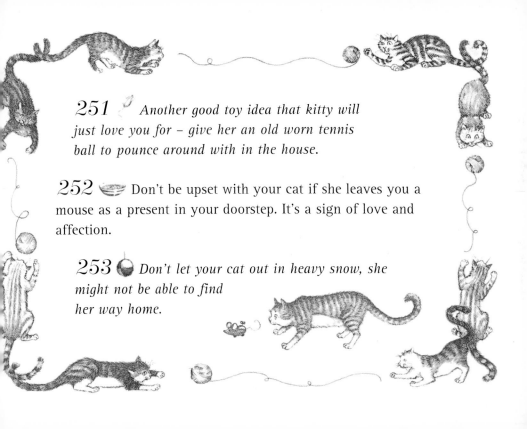

251 *Another good toy idea that kitty will just love you for – give her an old worn tennis ball to pounce around with in the house.*

252 Don't be upset with your cat if she leaves you a mouse as a present in your doorstep. It's a sign of love and affection.

253 *Don't let your cat out in heavy snow, she might not be able to find her way home.*

254 Always be polite and introduce your kitty to new company.

255 *And let her play with the company for a little while before you tuck her off to another room.*

256 Make sure that oven hot plates are kept covered until they are cool to avoid potential burns to your inquisitive cat.

257 *Once in a while enjoy your morning meal in the company of your cuddly cat and share a bit of your breakfast with him.*

258 Take the day off work just to spend it with your cat, and give her your pure and unadulterated attention.

259 *Be playful with your cat – on demand.*

260 Buy your cat the best fresh fish around and serve it up in a first cat-class style.

261 *Spend an evening at home with your cat for a change.*

262 Shower your cat with affection.

263  *Don't preach to your cat, she'll never listen. Be her best friend instead.*

264 Leave a new toy present in her bed every now and again.

265 *Learn these words: Ailurophilia – the love of cats; and Felinophile – a cat lover. They should be on the tip of your tongue, always.*

266 Don't interrupt a quiet moment of blissful purring for anything.

267 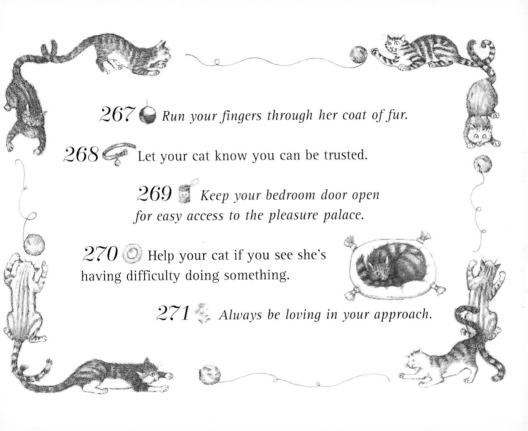 *Run your fingers through her coat of fur.*

268 Let your cat know you can be trusted.

269 *Keep your bedroom door open for easy access to the pleasure palace.*

270 Help your cat if you see she's having difficulty doing something.

271 *Always be loving in your approach.*

272 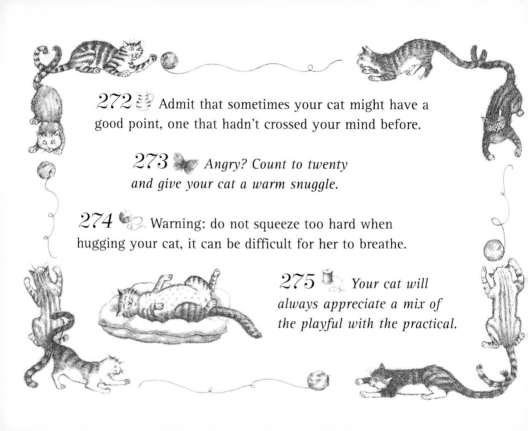 Admit that sometimes your cat might have a good point, one that hadn't crossed your mind before.

273 *Angry? Count to twenty and give your cat a warm snuggle.*

274 Warning: do not squeeze too hard when hugging your cat, it can be difficult for her to breathe.

275 *Your cat will always appreciate a mix of the playful with the practical.*

276 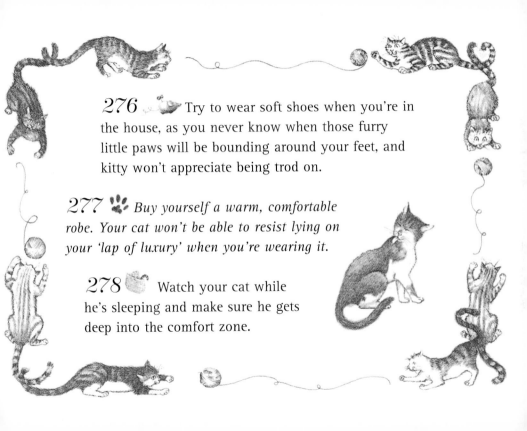 Try to wear soft shoes when you're in the house, as you never know when those furry little paws will be bounding around your feet, and kitty won't appreciate being trod on.

277 *Buy yourself a warm, comfortable robe. Your cat won't be able to resist lying on your 'lap of luxury' when you're wearing it.*

278 Watch your cat while he's sleeping and make sure he gets deep into the comfort zone.

279 *Don't place your cat's bed too near the radiator or too near the boiler.*

280 Devote time to your daily routine with your cat.

281 *Cuddle with your moggie in the evening after a long day's work.*

282 Make sure you have the number of an emergency vet who is available 24 hours a day if needed.

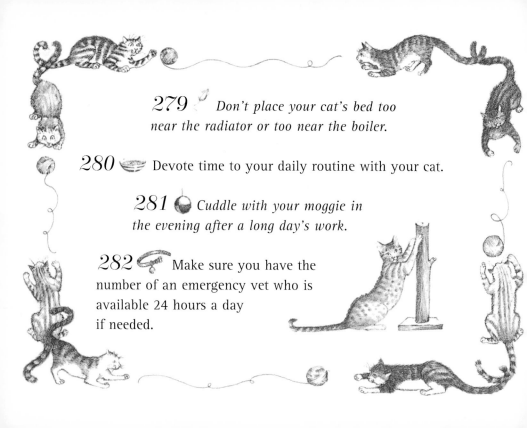

283 Be encouraging in all of your cat's endeavours. Offer a helping hand if necessary.

284 Fall asleep together, just be careful not to crush your furry feline friend.

285 Balance is the key word in all manners of treatment to your cuddly cat.

286 A harmonious home is a happy home where your precious kitty will flourish.

287 *Let your cat know she's your best pal.*

288 Tell your cat how much she means to you.

289 *Let her know you'd be miserable without her.*

290 Love means listening – listen 'cat-fully' to all that your cat has to say.

291  *Always be direct with your cat.*

292 Touch your cat often.

293 *Be gentle in all of your cat pursuits – never be rough with your kitty, ever.*

294 Try not to pick your cat up by the scruff of her neck. You wouldn't appreciate being man-handled that way either.

295 Tell her you think she's the best cat in the whole world. If you have more than one cat share the compliments amongst them.

296 Let your cat read over your shoulder.

297 Pick a song that will always remind you of your cat. For ever and ever.

298 Stick a bit of catnip in an old sock, tie the sock in a knot, and let your cat have some fun.

299 *Don't get angry if your kitty walks over the newly washed floor. Paw prints can actually be an attractive design element.*

300 Kiss your cat softly on her head.

301 *Give your cat an affectionate nickname, just for use between the two of you.*

302 Don't yell at anybody in the presence of your cat, remember she can be very sensitive.

303 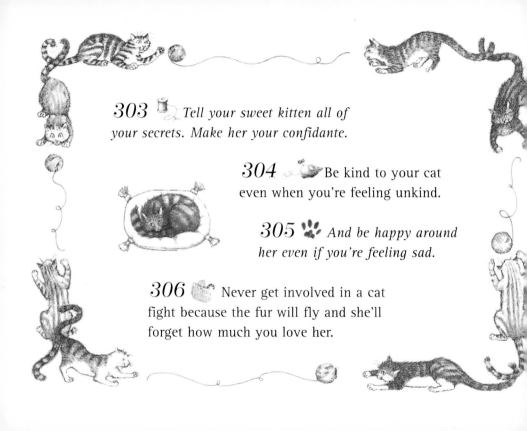 *Tell your sweet kitten all of your secrets. Make her your confidante.*

304 Be kind to your cat even when you're feeling unkind.

305 *And be happy around her even if you're feeling sad.*

306 Never get involved in a cat fight because the fur will fly and she'll forget how much you love her.

307 Be protective of snuggums, but not over-bearing.

308 If you make a promise to your cat, keep it.

309 Buy the divine feline something special on St Valentine's Day.

310 Be friends with cat-lovers only. That's what she would want if she could say it!

311 Keep breakable bottles out of the way of your insatiably curious kitty.

312  Always check under the car before you get in it.

313 *Keep your cat's sleeping area ultra-clean.*

314 Always treat your darling fluff ball as the cat's pyjamas!

315 *Be generous in spirit towards your cat. If there's only one strip of smoked salmon left, let your heart guide you to where it's best dispensed.*

316 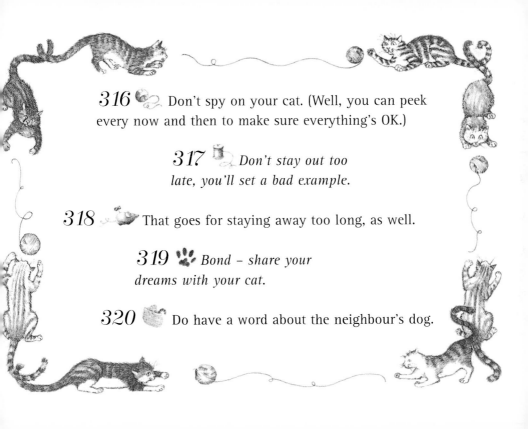 Don't spy on your cat. (Well, you can peek every now and then to make sure everything's OK.)

317 *Don't stay out too late, you'll set a bad example.*

318 That goes for staying away too long, as well.

319 *Bond – share your dreams with your cat.*

320 Do have a word about the neighbour's dog.

321 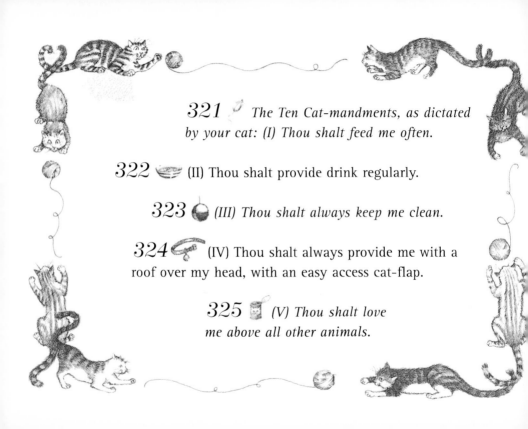 *The Ten Cat-mandments, as dictated by your cat: (I) Thou shalt feed me often.*

322 (II) Thou shalt provide drink regularly.

323 *(III) Thou shalt always keep me clean.*

324 (IV) Thou shalt always provide me with a roof over my head, with an easy access cat-flap.

325 *(V) Thou shalt love me above all other animals.*

326 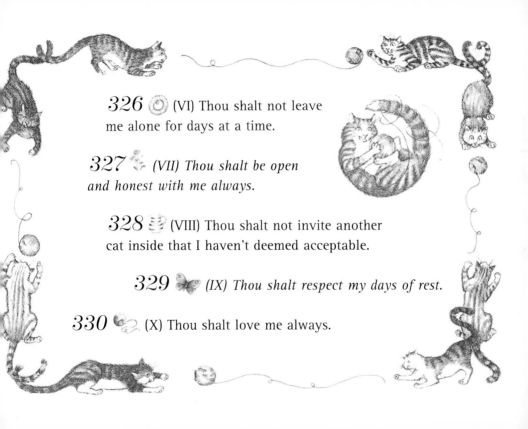 (VI) Thou shalt not leave me alone for days at a time.

327 (VII) *Thou shalt be open and honest with me always.*

328 (VIII) Thou shalt not invite another cat inside that I haven't deemed acceptable.

329 (IX) *Thou shalt respect my days of rest.*

330 (X) Thou shalt love me always.

331 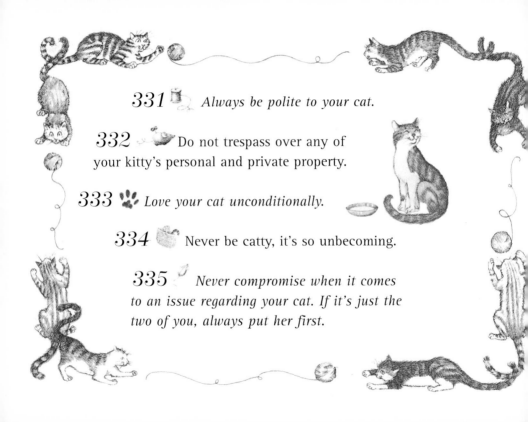 *Always be polite to your cat.*

332 Do not trespass over any of your kitty's personal and private property.

333 *Love your cat unconditionally.*

334 Never be catty, it's so unbecoming.

335 *Never compromise when it comes to an issue regarding your cat. If it's just the two of you, always put her first.*

336 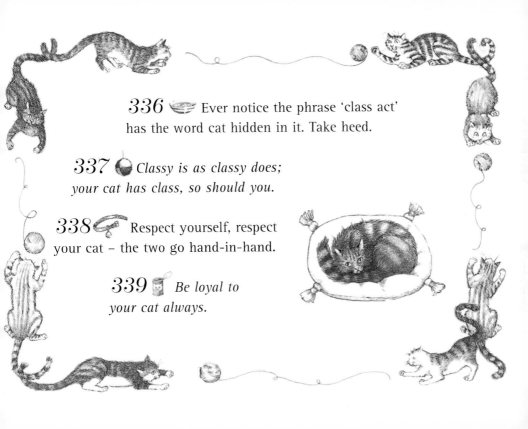 Ever notice the phrase 'class act' has the word cat hidden in it. Take heed.

337 Classy is as classy does; your cat has class, so should you.

338 Respect yourself, respect your cat – the two go hand-in-hand.

339 Be loyal to your cat always.

340 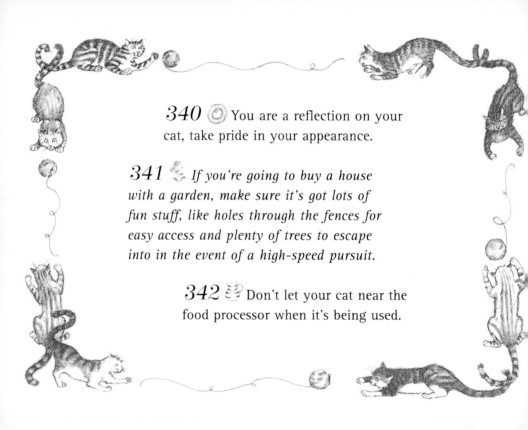 You are a reflection on your cat, take pride in your appearance.

341 *If you're going to buy a house with a garden, make sure it's got lots of fun stuff, like holes through the fences for easy access and plenty of trees to escape into in the event of a high-speed pursuit.*

342 Don't let your cat near the food processor when it's being used.

343 *Keep your cat indoors if the grass is being cut.*

344 And likewise, keep kitty in another room if you're vacuuming. No need to take any unnecessary risks.

345 *If you want your cat to stay clean, keep not only the carpets and rugs but your whole house clean.*

346 Keep the telephone cord tucked away in a safe place.

347 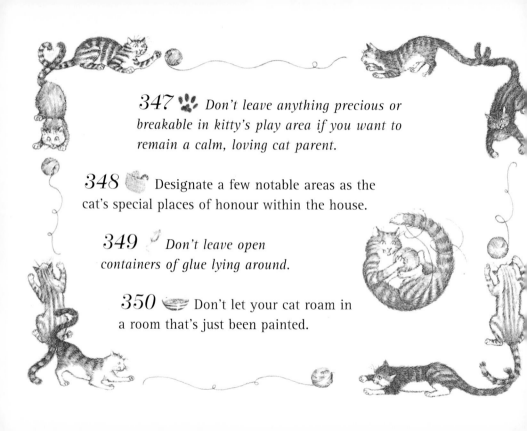 *Don't leave anything precious or breakable in kitty's play area if you want to remain a calm, loving cat parent.*

348 Designate a few notable areas as the cat's special places of honour within the house.

349 *Don't leave open containers of glue lying around.*

350 Don't let your cat roam in a room that's just been painted.

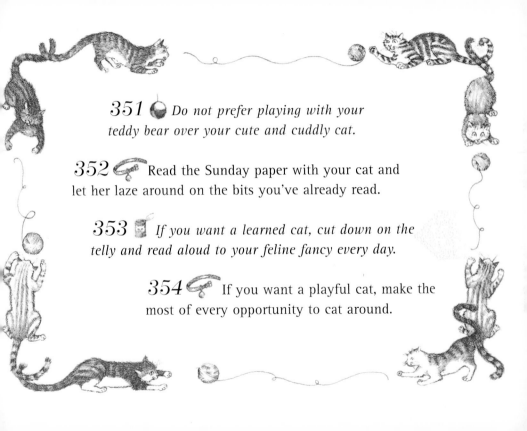

351 *Do not prefer playing with your teddy bear over your cute and cuddly cat.*

352 Read the Sunday paper with your cat and let her laze around on the bits you've already read.

353 *If you want a learned cat, cut down on the telly and read aloud to your feline fancy every day.*

354 If you want a playful cat, make the most of every opportunity to cat around.

355 *Go ahead and let your cat be frisky. Encourage it.*

356 It's OK, your cat will not get offended if you eat a Kit-Kat, she's a clever cat and may even want some.

357 *However, she will get offended if you eat cat-fish and don't share.*

358 Sharing is caring, but your cat might like her very own blanket.

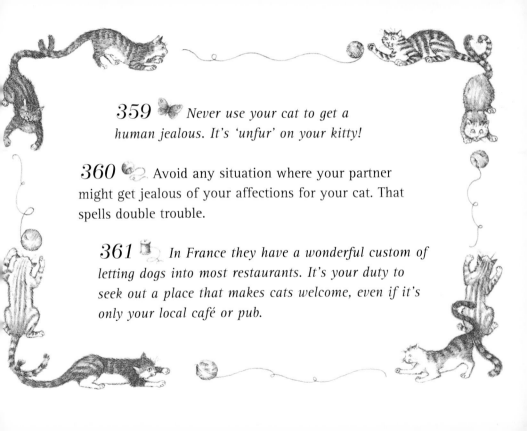

359 *Never use your cat to get a human jealous. It's 'unfur' on your kitty!*

360 Avoid any situation where your partner might get jealous of your affections for your cat. That spells double trouble.

361 *In France they have a wonderful custom of letting dogs into most restaurants. It's your duty to seek out a place that makes cats welcome, even if it's only your local café or pub.*

362 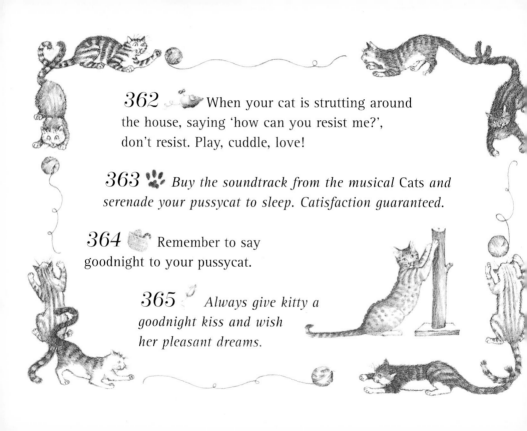 When your cat is strutting around the house, saying 'how can you resist me?', don't resist. Play, cuddle, love!

363 *Buy the soundtrack from the musical* Cats *and serenade your pussycat to sleep. Catisfaction guaranteed.*

364 Remember to say goodnight to your pussycat.

365 *Always give kitty a goodnight kiss and wish her pleasant dreams.*